Original title:
Conversations with Chlorophyll

Copyright © 2025 Creative Arts Management OÜ
All rights reserved.

Author: Juliana Wentworth
ISBN HARDBACK: 978-1-80581-758-1
ISBN PAPERBACK: 978-1-80581-285-2
ISBN EBOOK: 978-1-80581-758-1

The Spirit of Leafy Lullabies

The trees perform a leafy dance,
Whispering secrets with each glance.
In soft green tones, they laugh and sway,
Underneath the sun, they play all day.

Branches chat about the skies,
While squirrels pause to roll their eyes.
The breezes tease with gentle sighs,
As nature hums sweet lullabies.

Wisdom Rooted in Stillness

In a garden nook, the herbs debate,
Basil says, "I'm really great!"
Thyme chimes in with a spicy grin,
"Just don't forget who lets you win!"

The spinach school holds a class,
Where cabbage teachers let time pass.
Each leaf imparts a tale or jest,
But spinach claims it's simply best.

Abode of the Verdant Voices

In this realm where shadows play,
Grassy whispers make their way.
Each petal speaks of dreams anew,
While daisies blush in morning dew.

A wind-told tale of ladybugs,
They gossip 'bout their tiny hugs.
With laughter echoing through the glade,
The blossoms join the leafy parade.

Harmonies of the Forest Floor

Amongst the roots, a rhythm brews,
Mushrooms prance in their colorful hues.
In sync with beetles, they sing a tune,
While crickets smile beneath the moon.

Their melodies tickle the forest bed,
Where playful whispers often spread.
Each leaf confesses its witty plots,
In this heart where laughter never rots.

Under the Boughs of Understanding

Beneath the leafy canopy, so bright,
The trees swap tales, oh what a sight!
One claims to dance with the breeze, so spry,
While the branches giggle, oh my, oh my!

Squirrels join in with a chirpy cheer,
They ask the ivy, 'What's with your beard?'
The ivy whispers back, 'It's my green pride,
Keeps me looking sharp; can't let it slide!'

Ancient Talks of Mother Earth

In the soil, secrets buried so deep,
The roots share gossip while the daisies peep.
'Why do rocks sit? Not a talker in sight,'
Murmured the flowers, with petals so white.

The wind carries laughter from afar,
As a wise old oak tells tales bizarre.
'A worm thinks it's a king in its mold,
But really, my friends, it's just getting old!'

The Greenery's Gentle Rhetoric

Lettuce hollers out, 'I won the race!'
While broccoli laughs, 'You just took up space!'
The mint gives a wink, so fresh and spry,
'You leaf-eaters really make me sigh!'

A dandelion shouts, 'I'm the flower of the field!'
But clover chimes in, 'That's just what's revealed!'
With petals a-flutter, they start to debate,
On whose flavor's better, it's hard to relate!

Harmony Among the Herbs

In the kitchen garden, herbs have their say,
'Basil's the best,' thyme chirps one day.
'Try to keep up!' mint teases with glee,
But oregano snickers, 'Come dine with me!'

They rumble and tumble, with flavors to share,
Rosemary cackles, 'I'm beyond compare!'
But parsley retorts, 'Don't forget the zest!'
Herb wars are funny; it's always a fest!

A Chorus of Chloroplasts

In the leaf's cozy nook, they sing,
A joyful melody, oh what a fling!
With sunlight as their favorite tune,
They sway and twirl, under the moon.

They giggle as they soak up rays,
In their green gowns, they frolic and play.
A dance of light, a gleeful spree,
Photosynthesis, a leaf's jubilee.

Each drop of dew shares a silly joke,
Making the branches bend and poke.
Laughter echoes through the boughs,
As the world wonders, why and how.

With every breeze, they wave hello,
Nature's jesters, putting on a show.
In the garden's heart, a merry band,
A chorus here that's simply grand.

Green Notes from the Wilderness

In shady groves where giggles dwell,
The trees whisper secrets, oh so swell.
Mossy carpets host a lively talk,
As squirrels scurry, their tiny walk.

Vines twist like dancers in a line,
While ferns flounce around, oh so fine.
They share tall tales of wind and storm,
And how to keep their greens in form.

A leaf turns fast, it flips the script,
Tickling branches, laughter's crypt.
Frogs croak along, joining the fun,
In the wilds, the jokes have just begun.

Nature's stage, a whimsical spree,
Where every critter claims to be free.
In this wild place filled with glee,
Green notes sing a lively decree.

Nature's Infinite Dialogue

In the meadows, a yappy crowd,
The daisies chat, feeling proud.
With every petal, a story unfolds,
Of sunny days and secrets told.

Buzzing bees join the chatter fest,
As they bring nectar to every nest.
With tiny giggles, they tell of blooms,
While the daisies hum in pretty tunes.

The whispers of grasses sway in time,
They discuss fashion—who's got the prime?
With butterfly wings, they flap and tease,
In this chat, everyone's at ease.

Crickets chirp with a rhythmic pulse,
Adding jokes with a gentle convulse.
Nature's chatter, never does cease,
In this infinite flow, they find peace.

The Philosophy of Photosynthetic Living

In the sunlight's glow, the thinkers meet,
With leafy brains, a leafy feat.
"Why do we smile?" a sprout would muse,
"Because the sunlight gives us cues!"

To photosynthesize, they declare,
Is the wisest way to live with flair.
"Let's soak it up, don't be a slug,
Add water and soil, give life a hug!"

A wise old tree offered sage advice,
"Don't fret too much, just roll the dice.
Life's a breeze when you know the score,
Dance with the wind, and you'll want for more!"

So they laughed and hummed all day long,
In this green world, they felt so strong.
With every shimmer and bright green leaf,
They ponder joy—no room for grief.

Botanicals in Bloom

In the garden's bright embrace,
Petunias gossip, keeping pace.
Sunflowers wink in golden cheer,
'Why did the bee bring a souvenir?'

Lilies laugh in fragrant jest,
'Is that a frog? Oh, what a quest!'
Daisies dance, their petals spin,
'Who invited that dandelion in?'

Snapdragons snap with jovial flair,
'Careful, dear, don't touh your hair!'
Violets tease with shades of glee,
'Watch out, lily! A bee's on a spree!'

In this bloom of joy and jest,
Nature's whimsy feels the best.
From root to leaf, they all conspire,
To tease and tickle, never tire!

Reflections of a Verdant Mind

A fern with wisdom, wise and green,
Speaks of dreams, yet unseen.
'If I were a tree, I'd stand so tall,
And charge for shade, just like a mall!'

A cactus chuckles, spines all out,
'Summer's heat, please, no doubt!'
While roses ponder in their bloom,
'Could we start a floral perfume?'

Mosses giggle, clinging tight,
'You're wrong, no one lives here at night!'
But daisies puff, with smiles bright,
'Let's tell the moon to join our flight!'

In this garden's mind so vast,
Laughter sprouted, deep and fast.
With every leaf, a tale unfurls,
In the verdant world of giggles and twirls.

The Lullaby of Lushness

In the meadow where whispers roam,
A willow croons, 'I feel at home.'
With crickets chirping sweet refrain,
'Is that my song, or just the rain?'

A hyperactive vine scoots about,
'Catch me if you can, no doubt!'
While the grass blades shake, trying to sleep,
'You noisy bugs, come on, let's leap!'

The petals sway, a gentle crew,
'What's the buzz? A flower or two?'
A sleepy fern drapes, yawning wide,
'Goodnight, world, let joy be our guide.'

With lullabies sung in velvet tones,
Each laugh, each sigh, life overgrown.
In this lushness, joy takes flight,
As crickets serenade the starry night.

The Tapestry of Green Thoughts

In the tapestry where colors blend,
A kaleidoscope of blooms extend.
'What a matter—my petals are frayed!'
A zinnia sighs, 'Perhaps it's your fade?'

A rhododendron nods with glee,
'Who knitted this mess? Just let it be!'
While ferns discuss the latest trend,
'Let's grow out shaggy, befriend our bend.'

The ivy, like a gossip queen,
Spreads tales through the garden scene.
'Have you seen how tall that weed has got?
Next week, she'll rent a fancy plot!'

In this patchwork, life unfolds,
With hearty laughs and stories bold.
Every shade and every hue,
In unity, they start anew.

Heartbeats of the Herbaceous

In the garden, leaves do sway,
Chasing sunlight, day by day.
A thyme slipped on basil's dance,
While mint just giggled at the chance.

Petunias gossip, tulips tease,
As daisies try to catch a breeze.
A beetroot blushes, hiding low,
While carrots play a peek-a-boo show.

Sunflowers wink with golden rays,
And dance around in funny ways.
Sage rolls over, telling jokes,
As radishes pull funny pokes.

In this world of green delight,
Herbs and plants are full of bright.
When they laugh, we laugh along,
In nature's choir, we feel so strong.

Resonance of Roots

Underneath the soil so deep,
The roots are giggling, what a peep!
A tangled web of silly jest,
In earthy homes, they love to rest.

Little worms, they wriggle and tease,
Telling stories to the trees.
"Hey oak, your bark's a bit too loud!
You think you're funny? Not so proud!"

The grass below just shakes with glee,
At all the jokes from tree to bee.
Roots are buddies, sharing light,
As shadows dance with pure delight.

But watch your step, don't disturb their fun,
Or you'll be met with a leafy pun.
In the resonance of earthy cheer,
The laughter of roots rings crystal clear.

Harmonies of the Heartwood

In a forest thick with mischief's trail,
The trees exchange tales that never pale.
A willow whispers with a sigh,
"Did you hear what the pine did try?"

"Drop some needles on a squirrel's hat!"
"Will he ever get them out of that?"
The oaks and birches share their wit,
As each one tries to outdo a bit.

The heartwood chuckles, deep as time,
As laughter echoes in a chime.
"Why do you let the wind decide?
It's the branches that should serve with pride!"

And so they laugh through night and day,
In the woodland where fun finds its way.
The harmonies of nature's heart,
A perfect symphony, each a part.

The Green Thread of Life

A green thread weaves through every scene,
With laughter stitched in hues of green.
Leaves exchange quips as they sway,
While flowers join the raucous play.

Clover jokes with dandelion bold,
"Tell me your secret, oh how you fold!"
But dandelion winks, all aglow,
"Just toss me to the winds, off I go!"

The vines entwine in playful knots,
While critters dance with all their thoughts.
Nature's humor picks up the pace,
In this vibrant, green-filled space.

So let's celebrate this silly thread,
Where green life laughs and never dreads.
In every petal, leaf, and stem,
A joyous life, a leafy gem!

Dialogues Among the Canopies

In the shade, the leaves do chat,
Telling tales of where they're at.
One says, "I'm feeling quite bright!"
Another quips, "You need some light!"

Branches gossip, swaying wide,
While squirrels sneak, with seeds to hide.
A parrot squawks, "Oh, what a show!"
The laughter echoes way below!

The Language of Verdant Serenity

The ferns are fretting, feeling green,
"Did you hear what Oak just gleaned?"
"He's dating Birch, how very bold!"
"I hear they sip on dew so cold!"

Moss throws shade, quite literally,
Whispering, "I'm so comfy, see?"
But Sunflower beams, as if to say,
"I'm brighter than you, any day!"

Secrets of the Sunlit Understory

The mushrooms plot, in clusters tight,
"Let's dance tonight under the light!"
"We'll get the shadows to join in—"
But Toadstool winces, "Where've you been?"

Beneath the boughs, the grass does tease,
"Why so gloomy? It's just a breeze!"
The whispers drift, on mossy wings,
As ladybugs hum of fanciful things.

Musings of the Photosynthetic Soul

A dandelion dreams of being gold,
"I'm quite the treasure if truth be told!"
"But here I am, just blowing away,"
"Oh well, let's party – it's a good day!"

The ivy snickers, creeping near,
"I'm winning at life, oh dear, oh dear!"
While roots do wiggle, having a blast,
"Let's hope this good vibe will last!"

Musing Among Magnolias

Under the tree, we chat so bright,
Petals gossip as day turns to night.
Leaves giggle softly, swaying around,
While bees buzz by, their chatter profound.

Squirrels eavesdrop with curious eyes,
As branches dance, beneath sunny skies.
'Did you hear the rumor?' a petal will say,
'That the roses are blushing in bright array!'

Pinecones pontificate, wise and aloof,
Sharing secrets of the garden, oh so goof!
'Did the daffodils trip on their roots?' they chime,
While daisies chuckle, "Oh, how sublime!"

With laughter and sighs, the magnolias cheer,
Foamy blooms whisper, 'We've nothing to fear!'
As the sun bows low, the chatters don't cease,
In this floral realm, we find our peace.

The Garden's Gracious Gossip

In twilight's glow, the flowers unite,
Sharing tales of the day, oh so light.
Hydrangeas whisper, 'Did you see that bee?'
Buzzing around like it owns the spree!

'Listen,' the ivy sneers, full of flair,
'The weeds just bragged they're the lawn's best hair!'
Tulips declare with a dramatic flair,
'Give me some sunlight, I need a good stare!'

Cacti chime in, all prickly and wise,
'Oh, darling blooms, I'm happy to advise.
Stick to your roots and wear your best hue,
You'll have all the bees doing a dance just for you!'

The squirrels roll by, tail-twitching in glee,
'We'll steal the show, just look at us three!'
With laughter and glee, the garden's alive,
In laughter and whispers, the plants seem to thrive.

The Ballet of Verdant Voices

In the garden's hall, the leaves take their stance,
With twirls and spins, they invite us to dance.
The violets curtsy, their colors so bright,
While sunflowers stretch, reaching new height.

A chorus of crickets accompanies the show,
Each blade of grass adds a twist and a flow.
The daisies gossip, 'Did you see that pose?'
While ferns toss their fronds, in green interpose.

Cherries giggle, tucked high in a tree,
"We'll outshine the others, just wait and see!"
As the moon peeks out, the stars join the fun,
A grand soirée where all things are one.

With flair and finesse, the garden delights,
In the soft, swaying whispers of playful nights.
So when you wander, stop and take heed,
For nature's ballet is a wondrous deed.

In the Embrace of Green Spirits

Beneath the oaks, we lounge and we chime,
As chlorophyll spirits weave tales in rhyme.
Speaking in giggles, the moss greets the stone,
Sharing the secrets of roots long grown.

The tulips sip tea, with leaves as their cups,
While fig trees gossip about growing up.
"Did you see that patch of daisies get bold?"
"Oh, they're just trying to break the mold!"

The willow leans low, stretching roots on the ground,
"Let's hear it for veggies, their voices astound!"
Zucchini grins wide, wearing a playful frown,
"Carrots get shy when the beets come around!"

In this forest meeting, so lively and bright,
Each shadow and leaf sparkles with light.
So if you can hear what the earth loves to share,
Join in the laughter, it's all everywhere!

Serenade of the Swaying Grass

In the field where the green stuff grows,
The blades chat softly beneath the crows.
They wave and dance in a breezy jest,
Keeping secrets from the bug-turned-guest.

The grass whispers jokes in the summer heat,
Tickling the toes of all who walk their beat.
A tickle here, a giggle there,
Who knew they had such flair to share?

When autumn calls, they start to sway,
Composing tunes in a leafy ballet.
"Did you hear the one about the tree?"
Roots laugh louder, making quite the spree.

And as the sun dips down to sleep,
Swaying grass promises not to keep,
Their silly tales of wind and sun,
In a world where laughter's never done.

Whirling Thoughts on Nature's Breath

Amid the trees, where branches curl,
Leaves gossip in a twirling swirl.
"I'm the best dancer!" one proudly claims,
While another rolls its eyes, plays games.

The pines chuckle at the timid sprout,
"Join our waltz! What's life about?!"
But the little one shakes, feels so shy,
"What if I fall? Oh, my leaf might cry!"

In the breeze, they spin and sway,
Chasing clouds that drift away.
They exchange tales of raindrop fights,
While daring crows show off their flights.

The earth spins laughter; it's quite a scene,
As flowers join in, lively and keen.
With each rustle, giggles rise,
In this nature party, all are wise!

Heartbeat of the Green World

Listen close, the grasses chirp,
While the fronds of ferns do the happy burp.
The roots beneath smirk and scheme,
Sharing jokes in a tangled dream.

The daisies debate on who's the finest,
While the sunflower rolls eyes at the tiniest.
"Oh, bloom please, you think you're grand?"
"Watch me steal the sunlight, isn't it planned?"

In the lush, where humor sprouts,
Every shrub has its quirky doubts.
"Have you heard the one about the vine?"
"No, tell me! I'm sure it's divine!"

With twinkling dew and a playful tease,
Nature's heartbeat rings with ease.
Among the leaves, laughter flows,
In the green world, joy forever grows.

The Poetry of Plant Whispers

Underneath the vast blue sky,
Plants gather 'round, oh so spry.
Whispering lines of leafy lore,
Rhyme and rhythm from root to core.

Shrubs tell stories of wise old trees,
Of buzzing bees and frolicking breeze.
"I wrote a sonnet! Want to hear?"
"I'll share mine too; it'll bring you cheer!"

As petals giggle and right leaves twitch,
They weave their words in a playful pitch.
Nature's verses dance, sing and shout,
In every corner where joy is about.

So when you stroll through the verdant maze,
Stop and listen; the plants will amaze.
For in their whispers, laughter threads,
In every leaf, where humor spreads.

Green Spheres of Influence

In the shade, the leaves conspire,
Whisper rumors, never tire.
"Hey, did you see that bee, so bold?"
"He thinks he can dance, or so I'm told!"

A leaf fell down, it had a chat,
With a worm, who wore a hat.
"Old friend, you squirm, but what a sight,"
"Let's gawk at clouds and take flight!"

They plotted schemes and made some plans,
To hide from squirrels and those quick fans.
"Stay low, dear leaf, don't catch a breeze,
You might just end up in the trees!"

Laughter echoed through the grove,
In their green world, they'd found a trove.
With every rustle, giggles spread,
In leafy secrets, dreams were fed.

Rhapsody of the Leafy Realm

In the glade, where shadows play,
The leaves start jiving, come what may.
"Hey, do you think we're all just green?"
"I sure hope so, it's a lovely scene!"

They serenade the breezy night,
Dancing softly, out of sight.
"The sun's our friend, it's quite the star!"
"And don't forget, those clouds, bizarre!"

With roots that giggle, tales unfold,
Of talking grass, and sap, so bold.
"I dared a bud, it almost sprouted!"
"You silly leaf! What were you about?"

A rhapsody sang in vibrant green,
In leafy layers, joy was seen.
Each rustle brought a humorous cheer,
In the leafy realm, they had no fear.

Folktales spun in Photosynthesis

The sunbeams spark from leaf to leaf,
Spinning tales of joy and grief.
"Did you hear the grass was playing cards?"
"With ants, no less! Now that's hard!"

Mossy bards sang of ancient trees,
Whispering to the buzz of bees.
"Remember when the wind just blew?"
"And sent us all for a crazy view?"

They told of bugs with flashy suits,
Who stomped their feet in trendy boots.
"Oh, what a party, let's not nap!"
"Until the night, let's share a clap!"

Folktales spun in shades of green,
With laughter bright, we danced unseen.
From roots to tips, in joyful chains,
Nature's humor courses through our veins.

The Dialogue of Growing Things

In the garden, things were sprouting,
With chattering blooms, there's no doubting.
"Did you see that bug with fancy shoes?"
"He waltzes by, and makes the news!"

A sprout stood tall, with pride it spoke,
"I'm growing up, just like that oak!"
"But don't forget to bend a bit,"
"Or you might find you don't fit!"

The daisies laughed, their voices sweet,
"Why chase the sun? We're on our feet!"
"Let's have a toast with morning dew,"
"To every shade, both old and new!"

In dialogue, the whispers swirled,
Growing hopes, in nature's world.
A song of green, a playful ring,
Together, they dance, the joys of spring.

Forest Fables and Foliage

In a wood where whispers roam,
Trees gossip like they're home.
A squirrel claims he's seen a ghost,
But it's just a shadowy host.

Moss tells tales of the rain,
While branches sway and feign.
A wise old oak starts a joke,
"Why did the twig break up? It choked!"

The ferns laugh and roll in glee,
As flowers nod in harmony.
A chipmunk joins with a silly dance,
As nature spins in leafy romance.

Amidst the leaf and bark, we see,
Nature's fun in full esprit.
With laughter shared in sunlit glades,
The forest's fables never fade.

The Peace of Leafy Dialogues

In the canopy high, voices blend,
With a rustle and a glee to send.
"I'm the sass of the sassafras!"
Shouts a lively leaf with a bit of class.

The stout lilacs hum a tune,
While bumblebees buzz, making a swoon.
"What's green and sings?" a vine inquires,
"Elvis Parsley!" Amid giggly choirs.

Daisies tease the passing breeze,
"Do we talk too much? Please, oh please!"
"No way!" says clover, taking a stand,
"When you're this green, it's all just grand!"

In this chat of stems and trunks,
The air is thick with nature's pranks.
A peace found in laughter's embrace,
In leafy dialogues, we find our place.

Speaking in Shades of Green

In a garden where giggles grow,
Grass blades whisper secrets low.
"Did you hear? The sunflower's late,
He's stuck in traffic at the gate!"

A cucumber wishes he could sprout,
"Or maybe dance—let's turn about!"
With lettuce rolling, caught in cheer,
"Cut it out, you'll lose a leaf here!"

Pine needles nod, wise and sage,
"Youth is folly, turn the page!"
But young sprouts bounce like a joyful tune,
In shades of green, we're all in bloom!

As colors blend with fun-filled jest,
Nature's laughter, we're truly blessed.
The vibrant hue of life we glean,
In this playful world—so evergreen!

Secrets of the Swaying Grass

In fields where secrets softly sway,
The blades conspire throughout the day.
"What's the grass's favorite song?"
"The one about sticking together—never wrong!"

A dandelion whispers dreams to the breeze,
"I want to fly! Can I go, please?"
The daisies giggle and wink so bright,
"Hold on tight; it's quite a flight!"

They chuckle as clouds begin to frown,
"Who invited rain to our town?"
But puddles form and slosh around,
As critters hop to the wet ground!

Through bumps and jumps, they all agree,
Life's a party, come join the spree!
In laughter, they find endless sass,
Sharing the secrets of the swaying grass.

Secrets Woven in Vines

In the garden, whispers play,
Leaves gossip in a bright ballet.
Roots tickle soil, a playful tease,
While beetles chuckle in the breeze.

"Who's the tallest?" the sunflowers ask,
As beans climb high, a leafy task.
"Gentle vines, don't trip my toes,
I'm racing you!" a jesting rose.

The wind joins in, a merry tune,
As petals dance beneath the moon.
"Watch your step!" cries a cheeky sprout,
"Or you'll fall and dance it out!"

So secrets twine in laughter's trace,
Nature's smile upon each face.
In this green world, joy is rife,
It's all in the playful plant life!

The Silent Symphony of Photosynthesis

Leaves tap-dance in the golden sun,
While roots hum softly, just for fun.
A symphony without a sound,
In every green, new jokes abound.

"Chlorophyll, you're quite the star!
What's the secret to your bizarre?"
A tomato winks, all juicy red,
"Just soak up rays and dance instead!"

The air is thick with leafy cheer,
As ferns wave hello, drawing near.
"No negative vibes; we're all so bright,
Let's compost our worries; it feels just right!"

As sunlight pours, a laughter wave
Brings life, it's true, to all we crave.
In nature's play, we find our bliss,
In every leaf's resounding kiss.

Echoes of the Evergreen

Evergreen trees, standing tall,
Murmur secrets to one and all.
"Who stole my sunshine?" a pine will pout,
"Just take it easy; chill out, no doubt!"

The bushes chuckle, their leaves a-flutter,
As critters dance through twigs and clutter.
"Don't bark up me! I'm not your shade,"
Said a laughing willow, a leafy parade.

The breeze carries jokes, soft and light,
Tickling branches in gleeful flight.
"Can you feel it?" a nutty squirrel teases,
"Nature's fun, it's sure to please us!"

So echoes ring in the vibrant wood,
With tales of mischief, nothing's misunderstood.
Underneath a giggling green sky,
Nature's humor, oh how it can fly!

A Meeting in the Meadow

In the meadow, flowers convene,
With petals bright and colors serene.
"Who's the best dressed?" a daisy grins,
"Look at my frills; they're wins and wins!"

Butterflies flutter, a dazzling show,
"Ooh, look at us, we steal the glow!"
A bee loudly buzzes, "I'm on the scene,
Gathering nectar, keeping it keen!"

The clover laughs in a playful swirl,
"Each blade in this field is a jiving whirl!"
As daisies spin in a cheerful waltz,
The chaos of color's no one's fault!

The sun dips low, casting shadows long,
Yet laughter lingers, a vibrant song.
In this meadow, joy's the main theme,
Where every petal is living the dream!

Tales of the Mossy Ancients

In the shade where shadows play,
Mossy elders joke all day.
They tell tales of roots so deep,
While giggling in their leafy heap.

One bragged of how he met the rain,
Said, "She knew my name, not in vain!"
While another said, with glee and sass,
"I've got more greens than any grass!"

Life's a party attended by the knits,
Where every leaf joins in and sits.
They dance when breezes start to hum,
Their laughter like a gentle drum.

So if you wander past their show,
Just sit a while and let it flow.
For in the green, where stories bloom,
Lies joy, wit, and the softest plume.

Green Phrases in the Breeze

The wind whispers silly jokes,
Where branches bend like jovial folks.
"Why don't trees ever drink?" it asks,
"Because they leave them at their tasks!"

Leaves chuckle with a rustling sound,
Tickled by puns that float around.
A squirrel pauses mid-acorn bite,
Joining in on laughter's delight.

Banters of bark ring out like chimes,
As flowers dance, keeping the rhymes.
One says, "Can chickens even climb?"
And the others roll with joy each time.

Bright petals share their daytime schemes,
Wishing upon the sunlit beams.
In this green space, humor finds its keys,
Unlocking grins in the swaying trees.

Interludes Beneath the Arched Branches

Beneath branches where laughter spreads,
The chatter of critters fills their beds.
An owl hoots in a wise old tone,
"Who's there, who's not? I'll never be alone!"

A butterfly flutters, trying to tease,
"I can dance better than any breeze!"
Grasshoppers jump, with glee they'd strut,
"You think you're quick? Just ask my butt!"

A hedgehog rolls in with quirky flair,
"Excuse me, pals, I need a chair!"
While flowers giggle, swaying in mirth,
"I'd rather bloom than get the girth!"

So join the ruckus, lend an ear,
In this green jubilee, full of cheer.
For nature's fun is wild and free,
In every arching branch and tree.

Reflections of Nature's Palette

A painter's brush, so green and bright,
Strokes of laughter dance in the light.
Paint splotches from the bees' quick flight,
A canvas that twirls with pure delight.

"Why so serious?" the daisies laugh,
"We just wanted a sunny photograph!"
While violets pose with a wink and grin,
Their colors swirling, inviting in.

Each stream's reflection, a playful jest,
Where fish pop up for a silly quest.
"Catch me if you can!" they cheekily say,
Splashing ripples as they slip away.

So let's gather shades, let laughter reign,
In this vibrant world, funny without disdain.
Nature's palette, a masterpiece tall,
Provides giggles aplenty for one and all.

Between the Green Fingers

In the garden, plants gossip and sway,
A cactus claims it knows the best way.
The daisies snicker, leaves flapping so bright,
While the broccoli boasts of its head full of fight.

A fern leans in, with a whisper so sly,
"Did you hear what the oak said? Oh my!"
With roots intertwined, they form a big crew,
"Stop leafing us out, you know it's all true!"

The tomatoes chuckle, red as they glare,
Said, "We'll ketchup soon, please don't pull our hair!"
In this leafy hangout, draped in cool shade,
Laughter erupts, as the jokes are displayed.

So if you wander and find this delight,
Join in the fun, till it's turned dark as night.
Between their green fingers, the humor flows free,
In this riotous realm, wild as can be.

Nature's Green Discourse

The bushes gather for a weekly confab,
Where ivy insists it's the best to grab.
The saplings toot their horns with pride,
While the willows whisper tales that abide.

A beetle rolls up, says, "What's all the fuss?"
"Your leaves are so shiny, but boy, are they thrust!"
The poppies pipe in, with petals adorned,
"Don't judge us too harshly, we're just a bit worn."

The sunflowers stretch to the skies up above,
Asking, "Who knew plants could speak of love?"
With laughter aplenty, the green goes on,
While the tulips tease, claiming they've won.

In the heart of the grove, this humor prevails,
Among leaves and petals, the laughter unveils.
So when you stroll 'neath the foliage grand,
Listen closely, there's more than just sand.

Under the Shade of Wisdom

Underneath the branches where shadows abide,
A wise old tree, with stories, takes pride.
"Gather 'round, seedlings, come take a seat,
I'll tell you a tale about life and its beat."

The maple chimed in, with a ripple of leaves,
"Life's like syrup; it's sweet when it weaves!"
The grasses all chuckled, dandelions danced,
Their fluffy heads bobbing, all lost in a trance.

"Remember," said the oak, "to stand tall and fierce,
Even when summer's skin starts to pierce."
With laughter exploding, from each leaf and vine,
The lessons are silly, but sometimes divine.

So come sit a while, under canopy tall,
Where wisdom comes wrapped in humor for all.
In this shade, clever quips flicker like fire,
Amongst giggles and leaves, your heart will aspire.

The Emerald Exchange

In the park where the greenery thrives,
Exchange of tall tales, everyone jives.
"Have you heard of the herb that can dance?"
"It's the chives!" they reply, in a humorous prance.

The daisies discuss, with a flick of their heads,
"How to keep squirrels away from our beds."
The violets giggle, all shades of bright,
Saying, "We'll charm them with our sweet violet light!"

A sunflower bellows, "I saw him last week,
That pesky old rabbit, he's making us freak!"
But the roses just nod, their pride on display,
"Fear not, dear friends, we'll just bloom all day."

So wander through this emerald bazaar,
Where laughter and wisdom are never too far.
Inquirers welcome, for humor reigns clear,
In this vibrant exchange, there's naught to fear.

Verdant Yearnings and Gentle Murmurs

In the garden, leaves do chatter,
Telling tales of bugs that flatter.
"Hey there, friend, is that a snack?"
"Nibbles here, no turning back!"

Vines swing low, with a giggle and twist,
Whispering secrets, how could we miss?
"Look, the sun's here for a glow!"
"And the rain's another show!"

Branches join in, with creaks and cracks,
Sharing laughter, what a pact!
"Oh dear leaf, you're quite the tease!"
"Just watch me dance in the breeze!"

Nature's band, with roots in sync,
Lively chats over a drink.
"Sipping morning dew, how fine!"
"I think I'll stick to sunshine!"

Unspoken Bonds of the Thicket

In shadows deep, the whispers rise,
Ferns gossip under leafy skies.
"Did you see that bug take flight?"
"What a show, what a delight!"

Twigs perform a jolly jig,
Kicking up dirt, oh so big!
"Careful now, don't lose your hat!"
"Oh please, I'm all about the chat!"

Grass blades laugh at clumsy deer,
"Step lightly, friend, we're all right here!"
"You think you're smooth, don't you boast!"
"You're just a guest, I'm the host!"

The thicket hums with verdant cheer,
Muffled giggles for all to hear.
"Life's a dance, let's sway and sway,"
"Until the sunset takes the day!"

The Sway of Nature's Parlance

The trees exchange their leafy notes,
With swaying trunks and tiny quotes.
"Did you catch that squirrel's grand stunt?"
"He thinks he's cool, being so blunt!"

Petals poke fun, bright colors clash,
"Who wore it best? Oh, what a bash!"
"You know I'm better in the sun!"
"Yes, but I'm the one who has fun!"

Rivers flow with giggles and splashes,
"Hey, look at me! Watch my crashes!"
"Oh dear, don't take a tumble, friend!"
"I'll land on moss, that's the trend!"

In this lively, emerald sphere,
Every shade brings joy and cheer.
"Shall we gossip beneath the sky?"
"Only if you can take my high!"

Conversations in Canopy Shadows

The canopy chats in hushed surprise,
With fluttering leaves and blinking eyes.
"What's new today in your high crew?"
"Oh, just a bird that flew right through!"

Breeze dances around with playful glee,
Tickling branches like a friendly decree.
"Twirl with me, it's a lovely cheer!"
"I'll twirl if you bring on the beer!"

Ivy teases the creeping vine,
"Catch me if you can, just try to climb!"
"Oh, I might, but just so slow,"
"I'm not one for a hasty show!"

Sunbeams join the vibrant spree,
Lighting up each frolic and fee.
"Let's weave our tales into the air!"
"And hope the world will stop and stare!"

Interludes of Burgundy and Green

In sunny patches, leaves take naps,
Underneath their sunbeam wraps.
They gossip softly, where twigs align,
Sipping on dew and tasting the vine.

Bugs bring news of the garden town,
While each leaf wears its best green gown.
A dance of shadows, a flick of light,
They revel in whispers from day to night.

Wiggly worms in secret clubs,
Throwing leaf parties, with ample jugs.
A grapevine's wink, a dandelion's sigh,
Root by root, they cultivate joy, oh my!

In marvelous plots, plots for a tease,
Photosynthesis? More like leafy breeze.
With laughter in shades of green and red,
Dreams grow up, where the laughter is spread.

The Subtle Art of Leafy Lore

Whispering branches share tales untold,
Of sap-soaked summers and winters bold.
Breezy banter brushes the bark,
A bemused squirrel adds a remark.

Through knotted roots, the stories flow,
A leaf confides in a grounded hello.
Chasing the sun, they spin their yarn,
Painting life's canvas with each little charm.

Accidental hugs from a wayward vine,
Get tangled in tales, not so benign.
A raindrop giggles as it hits the ground,
Nature's echo, a silly sound.

Tiny sprouts debate 'What's flavor divine?'
Cabbage or kale, what a silly line!
In their leafy realm, where antics abound,
Life is a joke by the roots underground.

Persuasive Petals

A daisy desperate for attention,
Presents a smile, with pure intention.
"Look this way, I'm the cutest bloom!"
While tulips boast of their scent-filled room.

Petals arguing about aesthetic rights,
"Orange is the new pink!" they claim in flights.
Flaunting colors, they strut and preen,
In the garden court, they're quite the scene.

Bees bring gossip of flowery fame,
"Did you hear? Your neighbor's quite lame!"
A poppy chuckles, rolling in the sun,
In the game of blooms, all's fair for fun.

Oh, the petals with their playful schemes,
Chasing after sunlight, fulfilling dreams.
Each bloom a comedian, a whimsical sprite,
Painting the world with colors so bright.

Nature's Unwritten Manual

The rules of green, tucked in a leaf,
Not found in books, but under the sheaf.
Insect interviews hold the best clues,
From gossiping blades, nature's news.

With each tiny twig, they draft and draw,
A code of fun with a cheeky jaw.
Treetops plot as they sway with grace,
In the manual of nooks, join their race.

Chasing shadows on a lazy day,
Roots exchange tips in a playful way.
Photosynthesis, a luxury dance,
While critters jive in the garden's trance.

The whispers turn to laughter, grows wide,
As they share secrets of nature's ride.
In every rustle, humor blooms, you see,
In this unwritten lore of jubilee.

Rhapsody of Saplings

In a garden where the sprouts do play,
Little green giggles in the midday sway.
They whisper secrets to the buzzing bees,
Trading tales under the rustling trees.

A fussy fern complains of their loud cheer,
"Keep it down, you sprightly things, I can't hear!"
But the seedlings chuckle, dance in delight,
Their laughter echoes through the sunny light.

A curious acorn joins the fun and says,
"Watch me grow taller in a hundred ways!"
The saplings roll their eyes, shout out in glee,
"Just stay grounded, bud, like a sycamore tree!"

And when the wind blows through this leafy dome,
The saplings sway, feeling right at home.
Their rhapsody lifts the day with its cheer,
Nature's comedy, for all to adhere.

Echoing in Emerald Hues

Amidst the greens where the laughter flies,
A plant pranks a flower, much to our surprise.
"Why was the seed sad?" it giggles aloud,
"It couldn't grow roots to join in the crowd!"

The daisies laugh, with petals bright,
As the maple claims, "I'm the wisest in sight!"
"But what's with those squirrels?" a tulip quips loud,
"They're knuckleheads, dancing on the cloud!"

The bushes nod, their leaves in a flurry,
As the vines tease the trunks, in a bold hurry.
An argument blooms over brightness and bloom,
"I'm vibrant! I shine!" says a sunflower in plume.

Yet in this green madness, they all seem to bond,
In emerald echoes of laughter, they respond.
United by humor, in nature's embrace,
The joy of each leaf brings a smile to the face.

The Treetop Treaty

Up in the treetops, where laughter takes flight,
The leaves gather 'round for a summit at night.
"Let's make a deal to share all we've got,"
Said the mighty oak, with a jovial thought.

"I'll handle the shade and the gentle breeze,"
Chimed the palm, swaying with effortless ease.
"Just promise to drop some acorns my way,
So I can make snacks for the birds in the bay!"

The pines make a fuss, their needles all prickle,
"Don't forget us; we've got jokes that'll tickle!"
They spin tales of squirrels, of mishaps galore,
As lavenders hum, clashing leaf lore.

By the end of the night, the treaty's all set,
To share laughter, shade, and the cool sun wet.
And from that day on, in the treetops so fine,
The trees laughed together, leaving worries behind.

Language of the Leafy Lore

In whispers of green where the shadows conspire,
The leaves learn to talk, sparking playful fire.
"What's green and sings?" asks a buzz of delight,
"A leafy soprano under the moonlight!"

The ivy retorts, its tendrils entwined,
"What's a tree's favorite game? Please be kind!"
"Leaf and seek!" giggles an elm from nearby,
As laughter erupts, rising high to the sky.

The blossoms all join, fluttering with glee,
Trading their jokes like a light-hearted spree.
"You must understand, we're the greenest of jesters,
Sprouting puns with flair, we are leafy investors!"

With each playful jab and each hearty laugh,
They share tales of life—with a hint of a gaffe.
And through their leafy lore, a friendship does grow,
In the humor of nature, they flourish and glow.

The Voice of Verdancy

In the garden, leaves do chatter,
With gossip fresh, like morning patter.
They swap the tales of raindrop splats,
And whisper plans for dodging hats.

A pea pod jokes, 'I'm quite the snack!'
While daisies giggle, 'Watch your back!'
The ferns join in with swoosh and sway,
While sunbeams join the leafy play.

They sing of roots that tickle ground,
And make it clear, they don't back down.
A playful bough tells tree-top dreams,
While earthworms scheme with moonlit beams.

So raise a toast with leafy friends,
To verdant voices that never end.
In shades of green, all laughs reside,
A merry world where plants confide.

Chasing Sunbeams

Oh little sprout, you stretch and grin,
As sunbeams dance on your leafy skin.
'Catch me if you can!' they seem to say,
And you reply, 'I'm on my way!'

The daisies twirl in golden light,
Flinging petals, what a sight!
While dandelions plan to float,
On breezy days, their dreams will gloat.

The shadows tease, they play hide and seek,
While vines entwine, they giggle and squeak.
With every ray, they leap and twine,
In a game where sunlight shines.

So off you go, dear sun-chasing crew,
Where laughter grows in shades of hue.
Together you'll bask in the gleeful rays,
Creating joy in your green-filled days.

In the Shade of Understanding

Beneath the tree, a shady throne,
The leaves discuss what they have grown.
With roots so deep, they trade their lore,
While passing clouds drift and snore.

'What's your secret?' whispers the vine,
To which the oak says, 'Just a bit of time.'
They laugh at squirrels and their silly race,
With acorn plans that set the pace.

The grass comes up with tales to spin,
Of summer days when the fun begins.
While shadows stretch in a gentle way,
Leaving footprints of a leafy ballet.

So here they sit, in green delight,
With giggles and wisdom, oh what a sight!
In the shade, their humor thrives,
Creating smiles, where nature dives.

The Dialogue of Dappled Light

In patches bright, they start to chat,
Reflecting tales of this and that.
The hyper hedges joke with flair,
While petals float in sunny air.

'What's that aroma?' asked the vine,
'Oh, just the laughter of thyme divine!'
With petals blushing in the sun,
They spin a yarn about some fun.

The sun spills laughter on each leaf,
With dancing shadows, brief reprieve.
They tumble stories of bug and bee,
In dappled light, a jubilee!

So gather close, where laughter beams,
In nature's court, fulfilling dreams.
Together we'll bask in the vibrant glow,
As dappled light shares joy we know.

Through the Eyes of Elms

Oh, the gossip that we share,
Breeze tickles leaves, a charming flare.
Squirrels plot with acorn crews,
While we shade their silly views.

The sunbeams dance on emerald crowns,
We watch as nature wears her gowns.
Bees hum stories, quite absurd,
We laugh in whispers, seldom heard.

Rabbits bounce with leaps so spry,
We try to count, but oh, they fly!
These little dramas played on grass,
With roots entwined, they hurry past.

Sometimes we sigh—oh what a scene,
When raccoons raid our leafy green.
Nature's comedy, oh so bright,
In every shade, we find delight.

When Nature Pens Her Thoughts

Leaves scribble tales in wind's swift hand,
Pine needles giggle, a jolly band.
Twirling whispers around the trees,
As daisies throw shade and tease.

The clouds above draft clouds of fluff,
While insects chirp, just can't get enough.
A daffodil pens her poetic jest,
Nodding proudly, she claims the best.

Roots recite like old-time bards,
Sharing secrets in the backyards.
Oh, the stories they weave so grand,
In nature's book, we take our stand.

From rocky cliffs to rivers wide,
Nature's musings, her joyful guide.
With leaves as pages, all things bright,
We find our laughter in the light.

The Language of Lush Landscapes

In whispers green, the ferns converse,
With flowers' giggles, nature's verse.
Caterpillars in their silly dance,
Join in the fun, they take a chance.

Mossy carpets, a soft delight,
Encouraging critters through the night.
Oh, the banter of buzzing bees,
They jive with breezes, such a tease!

Grassy meadows join the tune,
Spinning tales beneath the moon.
While mushrooms chuckle, we can't ignore,
Nature's jokes, we want more!

Each shade and hue has something to say,
In a leafy lingo, come what may.
With every rustle, a clever pun,
Nature's stage—oh, what fun!

The Forest's Quiet Musings

Among the trees, a subtle jest,
The wind carries cheer, it never rests.
We ponder how to sway and spin,
With every breeze, our laughs begin.

Woodpeckers tap out a funny beat,
While hedgehogs harbor their secret treat.
A lizard lounges, basking where,
In nature's spa, without a care.

Gathered whispers fill the air,
In the foliage, life's funny fair.
Chattering squirrels hide their stocks,
As we join in, no need for clocks.

Nature's silence isn't so shy,
With every rustle, we can't deny!
In quiet musings, joy resides,
Together in humor, the forest abides.

The Wisdom of Worldly Woods

In a forest deep, trees argue loud,
Who wears the crown, the tallest proud.
Squirrels snag snacks, while owls make bets,
On who's the best, no regrets, no debts.

Frogs claim the pond gives the finest view,
While bees buzz in, sharing nectar too.
Leaves whisper jokes, it's quite the scene,
When roots dig around in their gossiping green.

Rabbits hop in, adding to the chat,
Discussing the taste of a garden hat.
"Lettuce is nice, but kale's gone mad!"
Who knew plants could be so very glad?

With laughter of branches, the day drifts by,
Nature's own jesters beneath the sky.
As the sun sets low, they laugh till they're sore,
In the Worldly Woods, there's always more!

Conversations in the Thicket

In the thicket, a trio of friends,
A grasshopper, a snail, where the laughter bends.
"Why rush?" said the snail, "Life's a slow dance,"
While the grasshopper jumped, took a daring chance.

Birds pull pranks, as the sun peeks through,
While thorns throw shade, pretending they're cool.
The bushes giggle, tucked away tight,
Sharing leafy secrets till the fall of night.

A wise old toad croaks a joke from the bog,
"Why do they call me a stupid old frog?
I have all my warts, which are quite in style,
But the lady frogs simply say, 'Stay awhile!'

In the thicket, where each tale's unique,
Every critter's voice is a bit of a cheek.
Embracing the fun, till the shadows grow long,
In nature's fair chorus, they all sing along.

Meditations of Moss and Fern

Moss sits back, enjoying the breeze,
While ferns spread tales like the softest tease.
"Do you know why the leaves turn red?"
"Because they're blushing from all that they've said!"

Amidst the damp, their giggles arise,
As the ground squirrels spin their acorn lies.
"Life's a great game, just dodge the rain,
And always remember, it's okay to complain!"

Each droplet falling, a sprinkle of glee,
Dancing on needles like a wild jubilee.
With roots intertwining, they share their thoughts,
Finding humor in all the plans life forgot.

As shadows grow long, the fun never ends,
Moss and fern weave dreams with their leafy friends.
In a cozy embrace, beneath branches that bend,
Time flows in laughter - nature's perfect blend!

Hues of Harmony in Green

In shades of emerald, mischief abounds,
Where laughter is found in the whispering sounds.
A tree winks slyly as the breeze gets bold,
While violets tease, whispering secrets untold.

Lettuce debates with a carrot so spry,
"Why grow underground? You're missing the sky!"
While cucumbers chuckle, rolling in the sun,
"Life's best in color, let's have some fun!"

Rabbits paint rainbows with each little hop,
While bees buzz by, never wanting to stop.
"Ode to the flowers!" the daisies all sing,
In hues of harmony, oh what joy they bring!

As twilight falls soft, and stars start to gleam,
In the garden, they share a whimsical dream.
With giggles in petals and roots in the mud,
The hues of the green grow brighter with love.

The Breath of Living Green

In a leafy chat, giggles arise,
The plants crack jokes, oh what a surprise!
A fern asks a cactus, 'Why so prickly?'
The cactus responds, 'To stay quite slickly!'

A sunflower winks, 'I'm the tallest of all!'
While daisies tease, 'But you're so prone to fall!'
They laugh and sway in the gentle breeze,
Rooted in laughter, as light as you please.

With whispers of nature, green voices sing,
Every leaf knows the joy that spring can bring.
A lilac boasts of her glorious hue,
While the violets blush, 'We all love you!'

So gather round, let the laughter flow,
In the kingdom of green, there's always a show.
Where stems and petals unite in fun,
A breath of fresh humor, under the sun.

Beneath the Canopy's Embrace

Underneath the good old tree,
A squirrel shares secrets, just for me.
The branches sway, with a knowing grin,
'Life's a game, let the laughter begin!'

A rustling leaf shouts, 'Catch that breeze!'
While butterflies dance, with the utmost ease.
'You missed it, dear friend, your joke was flat!'
The oak just chuckles, 'Imagine that!'

Ferns flirt and twirl, bold as can be,
While the shy moss blushes, hidden, you see.
Everyone's gossiping, right in the sun,
Nature's a stage, and we're all having fun.

So raise a toast to the bright green choir,
Each leaf a note, lifting voices much higher.
Beneath the big branches, laughter's the norm,
In this wondrous world, there's always warm charm.

Idle Chatter of the Foliage

Whispering leaves share tales from the past,
A walnut confides, 'I'm here for a blast!'
With acorns chiming in, full of jest,
'This quirkiness is what I love best!'

In the shady glen, a ruckus unfolds,
Bamboo compares who's the tallest and bold.
A willow sighs, 'It's about grace, not height!'
While the pines argue, 'We'll shine bright tonight!'

Conversations sprinkle like dew on the ground,
A melody of laughter in nature is found.
Flowers are gossiping, oh what a sight,
Spreading joy, as they bask in the light.

They jiggle and jive, in this leafy retreat,
Mirth dances freely, with vibrant heartbeat.
All's merry in the grove, where smiles are keen,
In the playful chatter of this leafy scene.

The Silent Symphony of Trees

Beneath the boughs, where shadows play,
A symphony stirs in a leafy ballet.
Maples tap toes, while oaks lend their might,
In rhythm, they sway, from morning to night.

A birch hums a tune, so sweet and sincere,
While the pines whistle songs only they hear.
The sound of the breeze joins in with a cheer,
Nature's orchestra plays, all coming near.

'Watch me . . . see my leaves shake with flair!'
The elm strikes a pose, all without care.
'Hey there! Lighten up! Don't you know?'
The willows contagious in their friendly flow.

So here's to the woods, a quiet delight,
Where trunks tell their tales, mornings to night.
In this silent symphony, laughter abounds,
With nature's music, true joy resounds.

Tales from the Forest Floor

In the dirt, where the snails do roam,
Mushrooms giggle, sharing a home.
Worms whisper tales of the sun's bright kiss,
While roots play tag, oh what bliss!

Ants march by in their tiny parade,
Telling jokes about the leaves that fade.
A chipmunk chuckles at a squirrel's slip,
As laughter echoes from each little sip.

The frogs croak loud, a raucous sound,
As crickets join in, jumping around.
They boast of the soil, rich and deep,
Singing songs to make the forest leap.

So here beneath the leafy throne,
Nature's comedy is fully grown.
In the whispers and giggles, life does adore,
The wild and wacky tales from the forest floor.

Conversations in the Canopy

High above where the wild winds play,
The parrots gawk and gossip away.
A sloth hangs low, grinning wide,
As branches giggle, trees can't hide.

The sunbeams tease the clouds up high,
"Are you going to rain or just pass by?"
Leaves rustle secrets, so sweetly told,
Of acorn dreams and the brave and bold.

The monkeys swing, cracking jokes galore,
While owls roll eyes from their stately lore.
Each twig and twiglet joins in the fun,
As laughter spreads 'neath the warming sun.

In this green realm, it's a jubilant show,
Where trees share whispers, and breezes blow.
A joyous choir, in sweet harmony,
The canopy dances, so wild and free!

Green Hearts Speak

Down in the meadow where grasses sway,
Flowers chat in a colorful way.
"Did you see that bee's crazy dive?"
"Yeah, it must've thought it could really thrive!"

Leaves flutter gossip, hearts all aglow,
As daisies tease the tall sunflowers' show.
"Your petals are bright but your stem is weak!"
"Still taller than you!" comes the cheery cheek.

In the bushes, the bunnies laugh,
Trading tales of their most fanciful paths.
A wild chipmunk's pun brings a cheer,
In their green heart world, there's nothing to fear.

With playful jests, they leap and twirl,
Each little critter in a dizzy whirl.
In this garden of glee, let's take a peek,
The verdant hearts giggle, so unique!

When Leaves Share Secrets

Under the boughs, where shadows meet,
Leaves whisper secrets, a fun little treat.
"Did you hear what the pine tree said?"
"His jokes are sharp, keep your head!"

The breeze plays eavesdropper, giggling bright,
While dandelions dance in sheer delight.
A squirrel drops acorns, giggling in glee,
"I can save them for future shopping spree!"

The ivy creeps closer, curious and sly,
"Tell me the rumors, don't let them die!"
"Fern said wildflowers have dreams to bloom,
Let's spread the word, brighten the gloom!"

Nature's own talk show, ripe with charm,
Each whisper and laugh keeps the woods warm.
In this leafy theater, laughter won't cease,
Sharing secrets, with joy, and peace!

www.ingramcontent.com/pod-product-compliance
Lightning Source LLC
Chambersburg PA
CBHW072128070526
44585CB00016B/1582